Beauty 2

BEAUTY 2

By
Marquita Graham

PUBLISHED by PARABLES
Earthly Stories with a Heavenly Meaning

Beauty 2
Marquita Graham

Published By Parables
May, 2020

All Rights Reserved. No part of this book may be reproduced or utilized in any form or by any means, electronic or mechanical, including photocopying, recording, or by any information storage and retrieval system, without permission in writing from the author.

ISBN **978-1-951497-13-2**
Printed in the United States of America

Readers should be aware that Internet Web sites offered as citations and/or sources for further information may have been changed or disappeared between the time this was written and the time it is read.

APPRECIATIONS

This book is for my oldest daughter, remembering the first time I saw you; I can still feel that jolt of love, and amazement at what a miracle you were. Now here you are, just a quick blur of birthdays later, all grown-up, and still a miracle! I've loved watching you discover your talents and grow into your gifts. Sharing with the world the light that's been shining inside you right from that first day.

I thank God for John Jeffries, for knowing the truth about trials, and temptations. I thank God for John's teaching how to be secure through suffering and knowing that I'm chosen of God. I thank God for Jeffries knowing the Believer's living hope. I THANK God for Jeffries knowing the wonder, and greatness of Salvation.

I want to thank my husband Mr. William S. Graham; In which is my favorite poet. For knowing how to conquer trials, and temptations. I thank my husband for the love for Christ, and his belief in Christ. I thank my husband for the joy, and glory that he brings, and for his salvation. I thank my husband for knowing the wonder, and greatness of Salvation. I LOVE William S. Graham Today, Tomorrow, and Forever! Every king must understand why his heart must be keen. Every king must keep love in his words, and soul. Every king must be proud of his legacy, and family is important, and last a king needs a queen.

CHAPTER ONE

Like a river to a waterfall, I call you giantess. Not because you're tall (All that is love is in you). Purple and blue, the hue of true. Soaked in a bucket and drained for two. Yours and mine alike waiting, to shine bright. Needing to be honest and true, I don't put my faith in people, I put my faith in you. You see light from eyes that have embrace the dark, you understand the elements of being broken by mended hearts. You separate reality from Illusion in a cruel cold world. You cherish the stone of will power as most people would cherish a pearl. You believe in fate but allow destiny to run its proper course. You let love flow through your heart, with your soul being it's feeding source. You fight for truth when all the chips are down. You refuse to quit on love and keep fighting each round. You show the world what madness truly should be. You sacrifice your inner self so that your love ones can always see. You hold time in one hand and pain the other. You show the world what means to be a heart from the gutter. You are divine, and that's something even you can't change. Your possibilities of love are limitless forever you will remain Beautiful.

I know sometimes, I look at my newfound life, with feelings of exhaustion. Discontent, unaware of how things will play out in my favor. When the truth is you can overcome the impossible with faith at the hem of your life. Just look at all the things you've been through as an example of your strength. You've faced and survived many battles before you were old enough to vote, which is a badge of honor. The trick now is not to sink back into comfort, and separateness. At times I know I am like a mine field, but I have good merit for my sense of troubles. Sometimes I have the world and at other times, I long to destroy it. I guess it's a creative thing. I was released from prison February 05, 2019. I had so many birthdays that I had to make up, to all five of my children. My heart was so broken that I was released six days after my first-born son, Shugg West-Jones birthday. Therefore, I set a lunch date for my daughter Imani Rucker 19th birthday, so I could talk to her about everything I've missed out on. I set a join birthday party for Essence, and Shugg at skate City; In which I posted videos on Facebook. My baby boy, everyone calls him babybro birthday party was a big party at the park, with all his friends, and cousins. I posted that on Facebook as well, I spent so much time with my children at the parks. That it had started the spirit of jealously, within my own family, and family friends. Due to my children having new clothes, and I was sold their old clothing at used clothing stores. I donated over twenty bags of clothes to the catholic charities. God has blessed me, and my children so much that I was able to get my amended taxes pay for by the church, catholic church does help those who help themselves. Currently my main goal was to restart by business, and to fix my children. I can do all things threw Christ, and god had to give me the strength.

CHAPTER TWO

My life story is a testimony for young women, and men. I wanted them to know that it is ok to make mistakes, life is a journey. Never less I didn't know that my first husband Mr. Rucker was so jealous of my first book titled Beauty being published that he would verbally assault me, every chance he could. Even on Mother's Day instead of him spending time with his own mother he waited outside in my parking lot for myself to go to church. Just to say I was ugly and fat, I believe he wanted a fight, or he just wanted to make me curse. I remined Mr. Rucker that I have a perm ante protection order that would never expire, and not to push my buttons, because the police were just one phone call away. "Did he care?" 's house. Of course not. A week later Mr. Rucker got so drunk that he assaulted our nineteen year old daughter, and his mother. The most embarrassing thing I believe could happen his mother, and our daughter had beat him up, and dragged him out of his mother's house. This really was a bad dream, because my perm ante protection order covered both of my oldest children Imani, Lovely Rucker. Since Imani was nineteen the protection order didn't cover her anymore. All the family sugar coated things for him for so many years, and his mother didn't even want to call the police. Due to all her complaints of arguing with her son, she believed she would be evicted. At this time, I was so upset at my own mother, because she moved my children in apartment in complex right next to Mr.

Rucker mother. I did so many powers of attorney, just so my children could be taken care of. The main one was for housing I put everything in my mother's name, and oldest daughter Imani Rucker. My main goal was too finding a house for myself, and children so I could move them away from the drama. That way my mother could go back home with my father, and my children would have them a house, and not an apartment. But at that time, I didn't know, that my mother didn't have any kind of attentions to move back home, nor return the things that I give her back into my name. This is were the spirit of jealously comes to play out. Mr. Rucker was homeless and not allowed to be within 100 feet of me. So instead of my mother having my back, and helping myself, and my children found a house. Every chance she got; she would call my parole officer over ten times in a month to try to violate my parole. Now it was already rumoring that she was in a secret relationship with my ex-husband Mr. Rucker. That caused me too get a life coach, and to ask the pastor of my mother church for counseling between us both to try to fix any issues that has caused so many issues in my life; In which I just wanted to move on, and take care of my children. God did bless me with my husband, Mr. William S. Graham, who helped me know the meaning of true love. Every chance I would get." I would tell myself when your mother, and father forsake you then the lord shall bring you up. What I found out about my mother was she was embarrassed of the things that I reviled in beauty; In which were very true, I did get a third degree burn on my leg as a baby. I did have separation of myself, and siblings. The main fact was the things that I did as a young adult that she didn't know about: In which god has blessed me with a change of lifestyle. I truly believe my life story is a blessing to others who have struggled, as a single mother, domestic violence relationships, and who has drug problems. God will help you heal and restore anything that was once too ken from you. What is love? If we don't earn it, or maybe we burn it. Like money than worship its existence later. What is love? If we don't fall for it or call for it like help. What is love? If it doesn't break us apart rip out our hearts, and leave us in the dark, like emotions do. What is love? If we don't write about it talk about it or look for it every chance we get. What is love? If we aren't blue, red, and green. What is love? If it doesn't provoke us, hold us, or make us scream. What is love? A joke of broken emotions. A sky that can't be seen, but you know it's there. A hug, a breath of fresh air. A stage of performance, a reason to go to war. A moment to cry. Something that leaves a scar. Something that makes you smile, something that strains your soul. Something you can't hear or see. Something you can't hold, something that makes you beg. Something that makes you flee. Something that takes your soul hostage. Something that sets you free, something that you can't look away from. Something that you can't stare at, something that never leaves you lonely. Something you can't forget. Something so beautiful, and hue. Something so beautiful, and true. Something that divides your heart into million spaces.

Something elegant and always new. Something with no explanation or expectations. Accept, what is love to you?

CHAPTER THREE

Thinking of my children today gave insight toward myself in a beautiful way. It's clear to see my husband, and I are selfish lovers. I know that sounds quite harsh to hear, but the truth is we have complex point of view on "love" altogether. It's not that we intentionally cast people out of our lives we do it to survive the impact we once felt. We do it sure we are never played, or mistreated. We do it because we don't trust love anymore, we would love to trust love again, but every time we prepare ourselves to go all in. Something pulls us away. It's like we are at war with love. I pray my tears are not ocean like and divided among many. I'm very proud of myself, and I find delight in the path of my journey to be the beautiful person, that Aim, marches on strong. I had to go to church a lot just to keep my mind right. I would go to my mother church twice a week, and go Colorado Springs fellowship on Friday's night bible studies, and Sunday evening services. Every time I would give offerings I would put, thank you for praying for me. My favorite scripture helps guide myself threw out the day. (PSALMS 91VERSES 1-2) He that dwelleth in the secret place of the highest shall abide under the shadow of the almighty. I will say of the lord, He is my refuge, and my fortress: my god in him will I trust. The main things that would upset myself, on a daily basic would be my children brand new clothing coming up missing. This was a regular thing that would happen in the apartment. I was selling shoes, clothing in my mother church, and my merchants, and merchandise would come up missing. This started to be a regular thing, it seems that no one wanted to see me win. At least they didn't want me to become a very wealthy businesswoman. The pastor of my mother church had to give speeches on blessing, and the things that I had in their church was for sell, and not a free blessing. Now I know this was explained a couple of times, due to language barriers, some of the members were from Africa. I thank everyone who had purchased my first golden sandals, especially sister Ann, and daughter Ashely, were regular customers. Even in grace, the devil would still have his present known. The spirit of jealously was made known. God has seen my struggles, and I know they will soon come to an end.

CHAPTER FOUR

In the middle of May I started back braiding hair, and doing weaving sew-ins on a regular basis. I would have most of the woman sign documents so I could put their pictures on face book, to help promote my business. A lot of the girls were, my daughter's friends. Imani had three of her best friends who I have known since junior high school, and Imani high school days receive designer braids. My youngest daughter Essence also has a crew of beautiful girls, that received designer braids, and books for mother's, also grandmother's. Just to make things known I had my own mother, also ex-husband making up the wildest of story's. Most of the rumors was   I was so broke, and I was homeless. God had to help me understand that the more I stood out, the more the devil acted out. I found out that my mother had memory lost, from being in so many car accidents, plus at times the spirit of jealously would take over my mother. I never had problem taking care of her, that was my main reason for being a caregiver. I forgave my mother along time ago for the things that happen to myself as child. I had to forgive my mother that way I wouldn't be bitter, and so I could move on with my life. My mother Charlette Harrington did get approve for long term home care, but I found out a month later. My mother had contacted the state local agency, and wrote a letter full of bible scriptures of why? She didn't want I Marquita Rucker-Graham to become her home caregiver. God has helped me to understand that

Charlette was embarrassed for anyone to found out that she need help, and that she couldn't remember things; In which affected her health. The devil would us my mother, in so many ways. At first, I praised my mother for wanting to get help, but soon as I found out that she declined. I just wanted her to go back to her home with my father; In which my parents have been married for 37 years. Because my father does in home foster care for adults. I really couldn't handle my mother at all, the sickness was in her mind; In which caused things to get so ugly, for the things that she would make up. Plus, I had to let her know, I must be the better mother that you weren't, it's very dangerous to have a person with mental health not to get treatment, and to be around, nor care for very young children. One of Charlette main problems was dealing with religion, also the church I wanted to attend. Made her very jealous to have my children attend another church, other than my mother's church. I just had to let the devil know, I never waited to the battle was over I shouted out loud every chance I could. Just like right now! If you didn't know that church people can be hater's, now you know. The devil uses them just like any other person, and the devil comes after them even more. I know one thing for sure, (Psalms 51:10-12) helps restore a right spirit within myself. Create in me a clean heart, O God; and renew a right spirit within me. Restore unto me the joy of thy salvation; and uphold me with thy free spirit. At the end of May it seem to be a problem every time I would braid my youngest daughter Essence hair; In which I hate arguing, since I'm a victim of domestic Violence. I hate loud yelling, especially in small spaces, and in front of my children. That is a sure know, know. What I couldn't understand about my mother, was she would repeat statements of conversations that I had with Charlette one before. About Essence hair, and I didn't want other people doing Essence hair. Reason being I didn't want Essence hair to get pulled out, and sometimes people does do evil things out of jealousy. Shared with my mother that before Essence dad, and myself had spilt up. Mr. DeAndre Turner would be cheating and doing drugs. While I was at work, and I found out that he would drop Essence, and my son Shugg off at different woman houses. Due to Mr. Turner being in a rush, he wouldn't get Essence dress, and He would let the women do Essence hair. I noticed after a while that my daughter's hair line was thinning out, especially her edges. So, I shared this with my mother Charlette Harrington, while I was in prison not to let people do Essence hair other than herself, and Essence's older sister's. Due to my mother's Charlette memory lost, she couldn't remember what I shared with her, threw all the things. Charlette would make it very difficult for myself, I Marquita Rucker- Graham to mother my children. I had a court hearing in the month of May; In which the judge shared with my mother, to let your daughter mother her children. I was told by the judge to put in documents, to take my mother's parental rights that I gave her of my youngest two children away. Since it seems like she wasn't trying to do the right things. Currently, myself, and my mother has the same rights too my youngest two children. Due to a divorce I had in 2017, my second ex- husband Mr. Turner gave up this right of his children in our divorce. I gave my mother custody, myself not knowing the issues that my mother Charlette was battling with her mind, and memory. Through it all, I know the wonder and greatness of salvation.

CHAPTER FIVE

Through it all know that you are chosen of God, know that you are elected by God. At times I would have temptations to drink; In which caused myself to overeat. I had stop working out at plant fitness. One thing for sure I never stop going to church. One thing for sure the devil never stops working either. I really thought things were moving in my favor, at this point. Charlette and myself had stop getting into, and Charlette shared that she really wanted to put my housing back into my name. Or even just add myself, that way she could help with my children, and I could help my mother without anyone knowing since she was very embarrassed of people knowing that she needed a at home caregiver. This seemed to be perfect for myself, because I just wanted to move myself and my children away from the area. Due to Mr. Rucker popping up any time he felt liked it and would verbally assault me every time he could. I just didn't want to have a generation curse arise. My mother's Charlette Harrington, mother Joyce: In which is my grandmother had killed my grandfather. My grandmother Joyce had done seventeen years in prison on a twenty-five to life prison sentence in the state of Indiana. Never less this was a trick, and I didn't even know it. Therefore, the devil was working in my own mother Charlette Harrington. My mother went to the courthouse and put a restricting order against I Marquita Rucker-Graham. That cover my minor children, aspect for lovely Rucker. I believed she was trying to copycat whey I wrote in my first book Beauty on how my perm ante protection order cover my oldest two daughters; In which my divorced had went by. Nerveless it was to keep myself from changings back in my name, and to let Mr. Rucker be able to go to his mother's house, since he could be 100 feet from me. Now since myself, and my mother Charette had the rights to my children, I had to put in legal documents to take away the rights. That I gave my mother in a 2017 divorce; In which my ex-husband Mr. Tuner give up his rights to are children Essence Tuner, and Dreundrae Tuner II. The judge in the protection order court set my court date back to Jan 21,2020. Just to give the judge in the divorce court time to modify things, so she can go by that judge's decision.

CHAPTER SIX

There are three things that truly leave me in a state of awe- diamonds, roses, and butterflies. You are lucky if you find one in your lifetime, if not all three. I love how they are created. Once I learned how they all were created. I grew a level of respect for each one. I grew fond of what it takes to be a rose. What a butterfly has endure, and what pressure a diamond must withstand. Sounds easy as we may say, but indeed it is not. Nerveless not knowing that I have had the devil using my ex-husband again. Mr., Rucker became my worse eminences, he had tried to assault I Marquita Rucker-Graham in front of my client Katie whom I do in home caregiver for. Mr. Rucker had gotten arrested for the violation of a perm ante protection order, and for domestic violence. I did get awarded victim Compensation; for loss support as related to the incident; In which Mr. Rucker was arrested for. This is a one-time payment up to 85% gross wages of the defendant for a maximum of two months (8 40-hour work weeks). The board approved payments for loss wages. Per statute, Victim Compensation is limited to paying a maximum of 30,000 on a single claim. I received the awarded letter on November 14, 2019. In all God has still blessed I Marquita Rucker-Graham. God is good all the time, and all the time God is good. One of my favorite bible scripture's as a special promise for me it is Jeremiah 29:11 " For I know the plans that I have for you, declares the lord, plans for welfare and not calamity to give you a future and a hope." At this time all I could do is pray; I would pray for others. Some of their problems can make my own problems look so small. I had stopped exercising, and I gained forty pounds. I know now that is a known, know. You always want to exercise, go for a walk, garden, mow the lawn, wash the car, clean the house, garage, basement, or attic. Long steamy baths helped my mind not to wonder, but to stay focused on the lord, and things I needed to do. I had to learn to go back to my hobby, I used to always read the bible, and I had a study group. But this this time I had to do things only for myself. I still did volunteer work; I did two sew-ins for free. One thing I couldn't even do at this time was to cry, but people need to know it is ok to cry. Cry to wash out your heart, and soul. One thing I did was, I dyed my blonde added some hair extensions. Just brighten up my appearance. If you look better, you'll feel better. I didn't know how my husband was feeling, about the things I've been through. I received a letter of courage. I believe in our beautiful bond which continues to grow more profound every day. We must be as solid as diamonds to be able to deal with the pressures of life. I want you to know you are beautiful, bold, and definitively brave challenging life from a different perspective. I miss you greatly, but I am very proud of you. The realest thing about our bond is we truly love the fact we are growing every day. My heart sees us in a different light. A light that reminds we are in gods hands. Thank you for all you do for us, and I find peace in our love. Embrace my confused heart show me what true love is. Baptize my forgotten star, marinated in your innocent kiss. Say this 'I will save you from dangers unseen by the keen eye. Let mw be your wings. Your beautiful wings, so we both can fly. Beside you, next to you. Words sounding complex to you, a true diamond. I am the vortex in you. With a gift that is yours to keep. I desire to watch over you as you sleep. Call me your protector of dreams, your diamonds buried deep. Even when you weep, I will be there. There to hold your hand. Showing you the essence of truth, and realness. Realness from a man, bringing fire to your heart. This I know to be true; beauty is only a milestone in time when comes to you. My beautiful diamond.

CHAPTER SEVEN

God blessed I Marquita Rucker- Graham with a book signing event at the Hillside gardens, for three weeks. I would sell my shoes, and book at this event. I would give out bottles of wine4 as a gift, when people purchased my book. I would have glasses of wine, chocolate, and other candies to the viewers of my emphasized book Beauty! God blessed myself with a radio contract, I had a nice-looking man by the name of Floyd Lee Boatright, offer me a SOCO RSS contract for media, and advertising for a basic sew-in extension package valued at $150.00. Plus, you also receive a copy of I Marquita Rucker's new book Beauty" a $ 10 value included with your package. All hair appointments will be held at the hotel suite for parties. Meat, veggie, fruit platters, and drinks will be served. Each customer is responsible to pay a 20% tip/gratuity. This was my first contract with SOCO Radio, Radio shopping Show! SOCO Radio are looking for new merchants to entice their listeners! SOCO Radio work on a barter system, and trade my services/ merchandise for marketing, and adverting! SOCO Radio has over 50,000 listeners. SOCO Radio broadcast on Blazing' 98.5 FM 11am-4pm Monday through Friday, 10-2   Saturday. SOCO Radio also 95.7 FM/1040am. My second contract was a certificate for $170.00 Retail Value for Cut   Color, and Style package. Plus, you also receive a copy of I Marquita Rucker's new book "Beauty" and a copy of William S. Graham's book "Leave the Door Open "a $20.00 VALUE included with our package. All parties will be held at a hotel suite for appointments. Meat, Fruit and Veggie platters and drinks will be served. Customer is responsible for a 20% gratuity on original value for staff. Make appointment within 30 days of purchase. I've had a great experience, great incentives, and customers are required to tip myself, and service providers, staff. I've received word of mouth sales from customers telling other about my great business.

God has blessed I Marquita Rucker-Graham with one of my back taxes check on October 09, 2019, this is one of many of god blessings. Even though I didn't get a chance to see my children on a regular basis. I would see my oldest daughter's Imani, and Lovely a lot more. I bought my youngest children Halloween customers, and would give money to Imani, and Lovely for their siblings. My children are my reflection. I know now that God has not giving me a spirit of fear, peace, love, and a sound mind.

CHAPTER EIGHT

I would have my dollar Imani Rucker be responsible for all money being deposited on PayPal, and cash out app. On Oct 01,2019 I was able to pay up a studio for my business, Shugg Sexy Lady's for two months. God has giving me the strength and has blessed I Marquita Rucker-Graham with money blessings, again, and again. Not to mention my pay was increases from the home care I work for as a caregiver. If you don't know God is good, now you know. There is nothing impossible for God, and nothing god can't do. There is nothing god want fix for you, and they're isn't a mountain high to high for God to help you reach. I had to learn to let go, and let God take all control of my life. On Nov 13,2019, I was told that my second IRS check would be resend, because I've changed my address to my business P.O. Box a trace of my 2015 check would cause the refund check to be resent out. WHEN I THINK OF God's goodness I can't even complaint, nor get mad, or cry. If I would cry it would be tears of joy. I've pay off my back business taxes off, and back money owed for student loans. All I can stay is I've been blessed up, and I will always keep my head up toward the sky. I will always keep a smile on my face, because God blessed I Marquita Rucker- Graham with grace. God has had my enemies become my foot stools; my two ex-husband Mr. Tuner even apologized for all wrongdoing that he had done to me and asked I Marquita Rucker-Graham forgiveness. Just to let me know his life wasn't even going right. Mr. Turner had so many domestic violence encounters and knew charges with the woman he cheated on I Marquita Rucker-Graham within our marriage. Mr. Turner explained why? People would be asking I Marquita Rucker-Graham questions about working for Colorado School#11. The reason being was, this woman had gotten a job after I resigned, and was fired for doing drugs. Mr. Turner stated he was homeless in California and had to have his mother come to rescue him, from living on the beach. Mr. Turner would wake up with a knife to his throat, and the woman trying to kill him, and herself. The drugs that the woman was doing would have her cut up her breast, and assault herself, and Mr. Turner. Now Mr. Turner stated that he was remarried to a woman, and that he was filing for a divorced. I asked Mr. Turner did he have homosexually sex with my first ex-husband Mr. Rucker, due to all the rumors. Not to mention the lifestyle that both of my ex-husbands had led, and they were hanging out with each other. Now Mr. Turner explained that he had worked for my ex-husband Mr. Rucker fixing on houses, but they were getting payed under the table. Mr. Turner also shared that Mr. Rucker was a homosexually on the low, in the closet, and he enjoyed being with woman at times. Mr. Turner new he was known as Mr. Rucker boo, and that I felt this was very strange. Mr. Turner also shared that he was married to a woman, born with a vaginal, due to rumors of trans gender, I had to ask very important questions. Mr. Turner explained to me Marquita Rucker-Graham that he knew his mother had gotten her hair colored by, I Marquita Rucker-Graham, and received copies of Beauty. Not to mention, a copy of my husband William S. Graham book leaves the door opened, FROM THE SOCO Radio Shopping Show. Mr. Turner is aware of how his mother feels about everything he has did concerning hanging around Mr. Rucker as weird, and very strange. I told Mr. Turner that I forgiven him, and I thanked him for explaining things too I Marquita Rucker-Graham. All I can do for Mr. Tuner was to keep him in my prayers, I shared with him that he had up to five years to take I Marquita Rucker-Graham to court for visitation of are children. After three days I received text message from Mr. Turner, and his mother that they both were moving to Denver, and they wanted to wait until our children were eighteen for visits, due to Mr. Turner giving up his rights in a 2017 divorce. I refuse to let the devil get myself down, at the end I still win. God has blessed I Marquita Rucker-Graham with a gift.

CHAPTER NINE

If you don't know like I know what the lord has done, for me. Now you know in Beauty, and in Beauty Part 2.; This is my struggle, and trumpet over everything. I want everyone to know that Tessa advocates for victims of domestic violence does help a lot with support, and counseling services. Because you can't move on with your life unless your able to forgive those who have hurt you. Let go, and let God take all control of your life. Even in the rough times I must thank God I've never been homeless, and I received a liable settlement. I want to let everyone know beauty is a life journey to becoming beautiful inside, and out. Beauty is skin deep, and my skin color becomes honey. I keep wine as a gift to promote beauty, and so women know how beautiful they are. Everyday I'm tempted, but god keeps me lifted. At times I could be blue, but I would rather be purple. That's a sign of royalty, and red lips are a sign of natural delight. Beauty works hard in every way, that's the beauty in hard work it makes you shine from grace. My life story is a blessing, and never a curse. If you look at all five of my children that makes I Marquita Rucker-Graham very beautiful. Just because my husband loves me so much makes myself beautiful. Even though I'm still on parole I'm still beautiful, because next year is a new start on my beautiful life. I don't compare my life to anyone else that's why? I'm beautiful. Always very lovely to look at, that's beautiful. Beautiful smile, and straight white teeth all make me beauty. With natural following hair, or extension, and makeup to enhance my beauty. Makes myself very beautiful, and very beautiful to stare at. Even though I transform myself at times, by losing weight, and gaining weight. I'm still very beautiful, and I shine like a diamond. I never lose my touch; I age with grace. So many people want to know my race, that's why I'm beautiful. I'm a queen waiting for my king to return home. That's the beauty in beauty. When you look at me what do you see a refection of my husband, and a mirror to my children.

CHAPTER TEN

All I do everyday is wait for checks that are over thousand dollars to come to my business account, that's the beauty of life. God will restore everything that once was token from you. My beautiful life is a challenge, and a blessing. I'm the spice, and the essence of my beautiful life. This is my life six months after I got released from prison, this is my battle that I won. Life is very beautiful, inside and out. If you didn't know my husband is my favorite poet. So, enjoy some of Mr. William S. Grahams poems about myself, and why I'm beauty. Like a river to a waterfall. I call you giantess, not because you're tall. (All that is love is in you). Purple and blue. The hue of true. Soaked in a bucket and drained for two, yours and mine alike waiting. To shine bright. Needing to be honest, and true. I don't put my faith in people I put my faith in you. You see light from eyes that have embrace the dark. You understand the elements of being broken by mended hearts. You separate reality from illusion in a cruel cold world. You cherish the stone of will power as most people would cherish a pearl. You believe in fate but allow destiny to run its proper course. You let love flow through your heart, with your soul being it's feeding source. You fight for truth when all the chips are down. You refuse to quit on love, and keep fighting each, and every round. You show the world what madness truly should be. You sacrifice your inner self so that your love ones can always see you hold time in one hand, and pain in the other. You show the world what it means to be a heart from the gutter, you are divine and that's something. Even you can't change. Your possibilities of love are limitless. Forever you remain Beautiful. One of my favorite bible chapters, that describe myself very well. The Song of Solomon Chapter 1:1-17, The song of songs, which is Solomon's. Let him kiss me with the kisses of his mouth: for thy love i8e better than wine. Because of the savor of thy good ointments thy name is as ointment poured forth, therefore do the virgins love thee. Draw me, we will run after thee: the king hath brought me into his chambers: we will be glad and rejoice in thee, we will remember thy love more than wine: the upright loves thee. I am black, but comely, O ye daughters of Jerusalem, as the tents of Kadar, as the curtains of Solomon. Look not upon me, because I am black, because the sun hath looked upon me; my mother's children were angry with me; they made me the keeper of the vineyards; but mine own vineyard have I not kept. Tell me, O thou whom my soul loveth, where thou feed, where thou make thy flock to rest at noon: for why should I be as one that turned aside by the flocks of thy companions? If thou know not, O thou fairest among women, go thy way forth by the footsteps of the flock, and feed thy kids beside the shepherds' tents. I have compared thee, O my love, to a company of horses in Pharaoh's chariots. Thy cheeks are comely with rows of jewels, thy neck with chains of gold. We will make thee borders of gold with studs of silver. While the king sited at the smell thereof. Bundle of myrrh is my well- beloved unto me; he shall lie all night betwixt my breasts. I love life, and I do live my life to the fullest, but I just want to give some information on mental. What is Mental Health? Includes our emotional, psychological, and social well-being It affects how we think feel, and act It also helps determine How we handle stress, relate to others, and make choices. Mental Health is important at every stage of life, from childhood, and adolescence through adult hood. Over the course of your life, if your problems experience mental health problems your thinking mood, and behavior could be affected many factors contribute to mental Health problems, including. Biological factors; such as genes or brain chemistry. Life experiences, such as trauma, or abuse. Family history of mental health problems. My life is a living seminal to others, I do have a family History of mental health. This is the reason for my book, just to let others know that getting help bis the best key. There is know reason to be embarrassed about anything. Mental Health refers to our cognitive, behavioral, and emotional wellbeing- it is all about how we think, feel and behave. Experts say we all have the potential develop mental health problems, no matter how old we are3, whether we are male or female, rich or poor, or which ethnic group we belong to. Almost 1 in 5 Americans experience mental health problems each year (18.5 percent). In the United States, in 2015, an estimated 9.8 million adults (over18) had a serious mental disorder. THAT EQUATES TO 4.8 PERCENT OF All-American adults. It takes enormous amount of courage to seek help. Mental Health disorders affect an estimated 22% of American adults each year. Millions of Americans live with various types of mental illness and mental health problems, such as social anxiety, obsessive compulsive disorder, drug addiction, and personality disorders. Treatment options include medication and psychotherapy. Posttraumatic stress disorder (PTSD), a type of anxiety disorder, can happen after a deeply threatening or scary event. Even if you weren't directly involved, the shock of what happened can be so great that you a hard time living a normal life. People with PTSD can have insomnia, flashbacks, low self-esteem, and a lot of painful or unpleasant emotions. You might constantly relieve the event- or lose your memory of it altogether. When you have PTSD, it might feel like you'll never get your life back. But it can be treated. Short- and long-term psychotherapy and medications can work very well. Often, the two kinds of treatment are more effective together. Therapy is the best goal possible; PTSD therapy has three main goals.

*Improve your symptoms

* Teach you skills to deal with it

*Restore your self-esteem

Most PTSD therapies fall under the umbrella of cognitive behavioral therapy.

There are five major categories of mental illnesses anxiety disorders.

- Mood disorders
- Schizophrenia and psychotic disorders.
- Dementia.
- Eating disorders.

- Deadliest Psychiatric Disorder: Anorexia July 12, 2011-ANOREXIA is the most lethal psychiatric disorder, carrying a six-fold increased risk of death – four times the death risk from major depression. The odds are even worse for people first diagnosed with anorexia in their 20s.
- \What is the hardest mental illness to treat?
- Borderline Personality Disorder, but what makes the condition even harder is that many people who live with Borderline Personality Disorder don't even know they have it. BPD is one of the most commonly misdiagnosed mental health conditions. One of the disorders that need to be made known, is Post -traumatic amnesia is a state of confusion, or loss of memory of the time immediately after atraumatic event, such as an auto accident. It is the loss of ability to form memories for a period after the accident, leading the individual not to" remember" a period after the traumatic head injury. My Mother Charlette has been in serval car accidents and does stuffer from memory loss.
- HOW TO HANDLE MEMORY LOSS

As we come to understand the potential severe long-term consequences of even a mild concussion, researchers are beginning to look more close traumatic brain injuries (TBI's) in the context of car accidents. Memory loss results from a hard blow to the head. There are several factors that determine your prognosis. If you have suffered memory loss because of a car accident. You will need to continue with your follow -up care, and legal action if need be. One thing

FORGIVNESS
THE ACTION OR PROCESS OF FOEGIVING, OR BEING FORGIVEN.

Forgiveness is the intentional, and voluntary process by which a victim undergoes a change in feelings, and attitude regarding an offense, lets go of negative emotions such as resentment and vengeance. (However, justified it might be), and with an increased ability to wish the offender well. Since I was a Victim of Domestic Violence I learn how to forgive, and never to forget. One reason Why I am beautiful, I learned how to let go, and let god.

Beauty 2